IMAGES
of England

BOURNVILLE AND WEOLEY CASTLE

A scene in Stocks Wood, Bournville, *c.* 1912. The area is also known as Camp Wood due to its proximity to the site of a former Roman camp.

IMAGES
of England

BOURNVILLE
AND WEOLEY
CASTLE

Compiled by
Martin Hampson

TEMPUS

First published 2001
reprinted 2002
Copyright © Martin Hampson, 2001

Tempus Publishing Limited
The Mill, Brimscombe Port,
Stroud, Gloucestershire, GL5 2QG

ISBN 0 7524 2443 2

Typesetting and origination by
Tempus Publishing Limited
Printed in Great Britain by
Midway Colour Print, Wiltshire

Lower Shenley Farm, in 1958, shortly before it made way for Shenley Green Shopping Centre.

Contents

One of the last trams to run along Bristol Road, seen close to Witherford Way, Weoley Hill on 5 July 1952, when the Rednal route closed.

Acknowledgements

My thanks are due to Birmingham Library Services (Local Studies, History and Archives) for allowing me to use their photographs. Special thanks are due to Cadbury Trebor Bassett (Sarah Foden) for permission to use the photographs on the following pages (where a refers to the top picture): 6, 10, 11a, 15b, 51, 52b, 53b, 68, 73-74, 76a, 78, 80-81, 82b, 83b, 84-88a, 90b, 91b, 93, 101b, 106-107, 113-118a, 121, 123a; and to the Bournville Village Trust (Diane Thornton) for the photographs on the following pages: 2, 4, 9, 11b, 12-15a, 16b, 17a, 23, 24a, 26a, 28a, 31, 32b, 35b, 36-39, 41, 47, 48b, 55, 59b, 60-63a, 64b, 66b, 67, 95b, 98a, 99, 108a, 110b, 111b, 112, 118b, 119, 120b, 122, 125a, 127a, 128. Thanks are also due to Martin Flynn, Paul Hemmings and archives staff for their help in the early stages, and to local studies staff for welcome technical assistance.

Introduction

Before the Cadburys came, there was no recognisable settlement in the area, Bournbrook (as it was then called) consisted of a few scattered farms and cottages linked by winding country lanes, the sole visual highlight being the Georgian Bournbrook Hall. The countryside was wooded and gently undulating, its antiquity epitomised by the numerous hollow ways, the bluebell glades of Stocks Wood (said to be a relic of the Forest of Arden), and adjacent Roman remains. When in 1879 George and Richard Cadbury moved their cocoa and chocolate factory from Bridge Street, Birmingham, to a greenfield site beside Bournbrook Hall, four miles to the south, they chose a location that was cleaner, healthier, and amenable to long-term expansion plans, predominantly rural, yet served already by railway and canal.

Renamed Bournville, the factory prospered, due to skilfully marketed innovative products like milk chocolate and pure cocoa essence. The Cadbury brothers consolidated their reputation as good employers, leading the way with above-average pay, Saturday half-days, and Bank Holiday provision. There were pioneering pension and staff consultation schemes, joint works committees, and a full staff medical service. The Cadburys were particularly concerned with the health of their workers; hence their stress on the importance of gardens and gardening, walking, swimming, and all forms of outdoor sport as an alternative to the confines of the factory. Bournville Works was especially remarkable for its open setting, surrounded by gardens and recreation grounds. But the importance of the arts and education was also stressed, the firm providing an excellent staff library and a concert hall complete with organ. Cadbury's later offered pioneering day release classes for school leavers.

Although he had built twenty-four homes for key workers at the time of setting up the factory, it was not until 1895 that George Cadbury bought 120 acres of land close to the works and planned, at his own expense, a model village with the object of 'alleviating the evils which arise from the insanitary and insufficient housing accommodation supplied to large numbers'. There had been earlier model villages for factory and estate workers; but Bournville differed from these in never being 'tied'; no more than 40% of its residents were ever Cadbury workers. It resembled the Calthorpe Estate, Edgbaston (where George Cadbury grew up), in its conservationist concerns. New roads followed the wandering line of old country lanes; mature trees and some fields and woodland were retained. Bournville was planned as a model for others to follow, offering a clear and viable alternative to back-to-back housing and its more monotonous replacements.

Work started in 1895, and for the first five years most of the houses were designed by William Alexander Harvey, initially principal architect and later architectural consultant to the estate. He established the essential character of Bournville, designing most of the houses in a rectangular 'country cottage' style, employing a variety of external designs with a basically similar floor plan. Wide windows directly overlooked large gardens which occupied three-quarters of the site. Like most 'Arts and Crafts' houses, Bournville homes were traditional in design but modern in fixtures and fittings; all, for instance, had a bath, at a time when many houses were still being built without one. To create the impression of informal long-term 'organic' growth, characteristic of a country village, neighbouring houses were deliberately contrasted: short terraces alternating with semis, and small plain houses adjoining larger, more ornate ones. The ancient bluebell wood, Stocks Wood, was retained, and the sylvan character of its original surroundings respected by the planting of many new trees along the exceptionally wide roads, which were always completed before the houses were built. At least one-tenth of the estate was reserved as public open space – outstandingly exemplified by the Valley Parkway, a pioneering 'greenway' allowing pedestrians to traverse the entire estate through riverside parkland.

The establishment of the Bournville Village Trust in 1900 formally ensured the controlled development of the estate independently of the factory or of George Cadbury personally. All surplus income was to be devoted to 'the extension and improvement of the Estate and to the encouragement of better building and planning elsewhere'. Apart from house-building, the Trust's concerns were to include schools and hospitals, museums, public baths and reading rooms. Many such facilities were concentrated round the triangular village green, which acquired something of a campus air with its infant and junior schools, the School of Art, and the Day Continuation School (originally intended for young Cadbury employees). Deliberately contrasting in scale, a homely row of half-timbered shops looked across to the junior school, whose spectacular Tudor-style tower topped by a carillon symbolised the key role of education in the community. Framed by the Quaker meeting house and Anglican church, the green stretched past the Rest House (modelled on the medieval market house at Dunster) towards Selly Manor and Minworth Greaves, two genuine Tudor buildings taken down and re-erected here in a pioneering conservationist project.

From the beginning, Bournville was a magnet for journalists and housing reformers. Harvey himself published a book, *The model village and its cottages: Bournville* (1906), and there were regular railway excursions to the village, where official guides and a furnished show-home awaited visitors. Henrietta Barnett, founder of Hampstead Garden Suburb, called Bournville 'the parent of the whole garden city movement', and the Garden City Association's conference at Bournville in 1901 itself bore witness to this view. Indeed, from 1901 the green and spacious layout of the garden village became the model for suburban housing nationwide. In Birmingham itself, J.S. Nettlefold's Moorpool Estate, in Harborne, was directly influenced by Bournville, as was the landmark 1930s council estate of Weoley Castle.

Between the wars, much of the major development of the estate was carried out by housing societies set up by the Trust, the most prominent being Weoley Hill Limited, formed in 1914 to develop the north-west side of the estate, across the Bristol Road. Nearly 500 houses were built, many designed to the requirements of individual purchasers. Beyond Weoley Hill, the rolling farmland centring on the ruined Weoley Castle, its farm and mill, was developed by the City Council as a 'green' estate, with a lake and parkland, wide tree-lined roads, cottage-style houses in good-sized gardens, and a large circular shopping centre known as The Square. The city's 40,000th council house was opened at Weoley Castle in 1933, and much of the city's massive house-building programme was stimulated by the example of Bournville. It was, therefore, appropriate that in the 1950s the City Council and Bournville Village Trust should have collaborated in the Shenley Fields Neighbourhood Development, in which the Trust provided 750 houses of various types for which the council had certain nomination rights on tenancies.

Throughout its history, the Trust has been willing to experiment – with self-building schemes, new building materials, solar housing, homes for particular groups (e.g. retired teachers, single professional women, single mothers, the physically and mentally handicapped). Housing developments continued into the 1990s – often utilising the landscaping of earlier private estates. The last remaining land used was at 'The Davids', the former home of Laurence Cadbury, where the estate was sold to a private developer, enabling the Trust to raise a large capital sum for investment in social housing elsewhere.

Bournville has educational establishments of many kinds, the most notable being the Selly Oak Colleges, grouped along the Bristol Road between Bournville and Weoley Hill. Starting with Woodbrooke, George Cadbury's former home, which he founded in 1903 as a Quaker study centre, they now form a loose affiliation of religious institutions, whose principal concerns include international relations and multi-faith studies, missionary work and teacher training.

True to its famous wartime report, *When we build again* (1941), the Trust has continued to exercise an international influence on housing and town planning generally. Now containing 7,800 homes on 1,000 acres of land, with 100 acres of parks and open spaces, it maintains an exemplary and practical role, with some direct local authority involvement, most recently at Telford, Shropshire, and Bordesley Village, Birmingham.

Martin Hampson
July 2001

One
Rural Past

Woodbrooke Farm, Bournville, in 1958, shortly before its demolition. The West Midlands Police Headquarters now occupies the site.

Bournbrook Cottage, in 1879, shortly before the construction of Bournville Works. When the Cadburys first came here, only this cottage and Bournbrook Hall and Farm across the road occupied the site. The administrative offices and staff entrances were later sited along this stretch of Bournville Lane.

Bournbrook Hall Farm, in 1890. The farm stood at the rear of Bournbrook Hall, between Bournville Lane and the Almshouses.

Hay Green Farm, Bournville, was mentioned in records as early as 1540; but was pulled down in 1927/28 to make way for housing. It is seen here around 1920.

Hay Green Lane in 1905, before development.

Hole Lane in the 1920s.

A Rowheath Farm outbuilding, seen in 1983. The Rowheath Farm estate was purchased jointly by Cadbury's and the Bournville Village Trust in 1911, and subsequently developed for recreational and housing purposes. Some of the farm buildings, on Selly Oak Road, survive as private residences.

Harvesting at Middle Park Farm, at the start of the Weoley Hill development, c. 1920.

Middle Park Farm, which occupied land between Bristol Road and Swarthmore Road, was first mentioned in the 1851 census. This harvest scene dates from around 1920. Until the farm was demolished in 1958, cows were led regularly across the Bristol Road. The farmland is now occupied by the Bournville College of Further Education and the Weoley Hill Estate.

Working on Middle Park Farm in 1936.

The Valley Parkway, Bournville, in 1932, before the construction of the Model Yachting Pool.

These seventeenth-century cottages on Cob Lane, Bournville, are the oldest houses on the estate, seen here in 1985. Originally homes for workers at Woodbrooke Farm, they contain ceiling beams that are said to have once been ship's timbers.

Weoley Hill before development, *c.* 1920.

Lower Shenley Farm, seen in 1958, shortly before demolition, was first mentioned in 1841. The site is now occupied by Shenley Green Shopping Centre, St David's church, and surrounding houses, maisonettes and flats. Green Meadow School stands close to the site of the original farmyard.

Shenley Hill in 1935.

Weoley Park Road before development, 1933.

Princethorpe Road from Weoley Park Road, 1931.

The junction of Princethorpe Road and Weoley Castle Road, 1931.

The junction of Shenley Fields Road and Weoley Park Road, 1931.

Barnes Hill, looking north, before the housing developments, 1931.

Weoley Castle Farm and Mill Pool, in 1932, were on Alwold Road, adjacent to the Castle ruins.

Weoley Castle farmhouse and garden, 1932.

Weoley Castle Farm, showing the entrance to the castle ruins, in 1950.

Weoley Castle Mill and pool, 1932.

The interior of Weoley Castle Mill, 1932.

Two
Street Scenes and Landmarks

Bournville Junior School and Carillon, with the infants' school in the foreground, *c*. 1910.

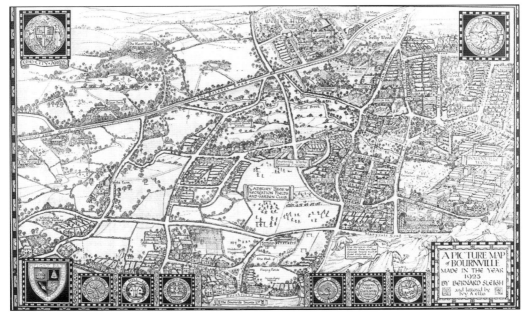

A picture map of Bournville, drawn by Bernard Sleigh in 1923, and showing a still predominantly rural scene. References are made to the various housing societies which had worked with the Trust in recent years.

The junior school and Carillon, Bournville, seen in 1949. Built at the personal expense of George and Elizabeth Cadbury, and designed by William Alexander Harvey in 1902-05, it resembles a miniature Oxford college with its massive Tudor-style tower complete with oriel window and staircase turret. The tower was functional as well as ornamental, housing a library and laboratory, while the view from the top was used in local geography lessons, a map and compass being provided. The cupola surmounting the tower contains a carillon of forty-eight bells, inspired by the carillon at Bruges which George Cadbury admired.

24

View from the Carillon in 1949, looking past Bournville Meeting House towards the village green and Stocks Wood. The carillon features regularly in concerts as well as chiming the hours; it is perhaps symbolic of the high importance accorded by the Cadburys to education that the bell tower is attached to the junior school rather than the church.

Bournville station and Mary Vale Road, with Cadbury's factory in the background, c. 1920. The Birmingham West Suburban Railway opened in 1876, and its presence undoubtedly influenced the Cadburys choice of site in 1879. From 1884 to 1963, Cadbury's ran their own private railway (which they modestly termed a siding), consisting of 4.5 miles of track serving all parts of the works, the layout being almost circular, designed for speedy and efficient reception and despatch. The firm used their own purpose-built tank engines; bulk traffic consisted chiefly of cocoa beans delivered direct from Liverpool Docks.

Bournville village green in 1910, at an early stage before the building of the Rest House or Day Continuation School.

The Rest House, Bournville Green, in 1949. Built in 1914 by W.A. Harvey, it is modelled on the late sixteenth-century yarn market at Dunster in Somerset, and was a gift from Cadbury employees worldwide to commemorate the silver wedding anniversary of George and Elizabeth Cadbury. To enhance its ancient appearance, it was built of brick from old buildings in Bruges. Inside there are carved stone panels recording events in the development of Cadbury Works and the village.

Bournville Green and the Rest House in the late 1950s, showing W.A. Harvey's junior school and Carillon at the rear. The green is the scene of a unique event on Christmas Eve, when there is open-air carol singing lit by lanterns and accompanied by the Carillon. The Rest House now serves as a craft shop and information centre.

The village green and Rest House, c. 1960. Bedford Tyler's 'country town style' row of shops is at the rear.

Shops on Bournville Green, *c.* 1927. They were designed by Bedford Tyler, another important Bournville Trust architect, and built between 1905 and 1908. The Trust allows shops to operate only in specially designated areas, rejecting piecemeal developments.

The same shops in 1949, looking along Sycamore Road towards Linden Road. Characteristic of Bournville are the cottage scale and the symmetrical overall design, making the row look like one large building, with a central gable containing an oriel window.

Sycamore Road houses in 1965, adjoining the village green, and exemplifying W.A. Harvey's varied 'cottage style' of housing.

The Bournville Triangle, the junction of Sycamore, Willow and Laburnum Roads, *c.* 1910. Most of the early Bournville roads were named after trees – appropriately, for a garden suburb.

Mary Vale Road, 1949. The first Bournville estate houses were built here, on the north side, in 1895. They were designed by Alfred Walker, later he would become estate surveyor. The later houses were designed by W.A. Harvey.

Mary Vale Road, *c*. 1920. This was on the other side of Linden Road, showing on the right the Tudor-style shops designed by W.A. Harvey in 1897, the first shops to be built in Bournville.

A closer view of the first Bournville shops, on Mary Vale Road, *c*. 1905.

More distinctively designed shops, also by Harvey, farther along Mary Vale Road, *c*. 1905.

Beech Road, looking towards Bournville Park, with Thorn Road beyond, *c.* 1920.

The east side of Thorn Road, beyond the park, seen in the early 1900s. The two roads are connected by a footpath through the park.

The junction of Selly Oak Road and Bournville Lane, seen in 1925, before Bournville Lane was cut through to Bristol Road on the left. Part of Rowheath Playing Fields can be seen beyond the railings.

Selly Oak Road from Mary Vale Road, looking south, in 1925.

The Bristol Road footbridge, seen in 1969, soon after opening. Linking Bournville and Weoley Hill, it not only fulfils this practical purpose, but also forms a striking 'gateway' to Bournville for travellers along the Bristol Road.

A tram serving the same area, at the foot of Griffins Hill, Bristol Road, in 1931.

Tram on Griffins Hill, Bristol Road, 1931.

Newly completed houses on Middle Park Road, Weoley Hill, 13 December 1929.

Weoley Hill from Green Meadow Road, beside the church, in 1937, as the estate neared completion. Weoley Hill Limited was founded in 1914 to develop land across the Bristol Road north-west of the original Bournville Village. Nearly 500 houses were built and sold on 99-year leases between the wars. Weoley Hill centres on the Valley Parkway, which links Weoley Castle with Bournville and contains extensive sports grounds. It has a church and village hall and post office, but no shops – at the request of local residents.

Weoley Hill Village Hall, 1933.

Fox Hill, Weoley Hill, in 1933. While retaining the green and spacious character of the original Bournville estate, Weoley Hill was more informally planned, using natural features and contours and allowing roads to wind uphill, following the lie of the land. Originally intended for young first-time buyers and advertised as 'conveniently close to the city centre by tram … and having electric lighting', it became an increasingly attractive residential suburb during the 1930s, some of the later houses to be built were quite large.

Fox Hill, Weoley Hill, again in 1933, showing the large gardens and cottage style of the houses, characteristics shared with the original Bournville.

Fox Hill in the 1920s.

Fox Hill Close, Weoley Hill, in 1933.

Spiceland Road, Yew Tree Farm Estate, in 1963. Part of the post-war Shenley Fields development, the estate is named after the former Yew Tree Farm, which stood on the western side of Shenley Lane, opposite Lower Shenley Farm, and was pulled down in the 1950s. When the first tenants moved in, the gardens were not hedged, and cows used to wander in from the fields.

Spiceland Road, again in 1963 – a park-like setting recalling Bournville.

Quarry Road, Weoley Castle, under construction in 1931. This scene is viewed from opposite Stoneton Grove, looking towards Shenley Fields Road.

Shenley Fields Road, west of Middle Park Road, 1935.

St David's church and Shenley Green in 1970. Lower Shenley Farm stood on the site until 1958.

Green Meadow Road, Shenley Fields, in 1968, showing the wide variety of housing made available. The Shenley Fields Neighbourhood Development, undertaken in the 1950s and early 1960s, was a joint project of Birmingham City Council and Bournville Village Trust, with the Trust planning and building the estate but offering the council a number of tenancies in return for financial assistance. The estate contained housing suitable for all ages, including blocks of combined flats and maisonettes, and semi-detached houses capable of being converted into flats if the need arose. In all, 750 homes were provided, at a time when the city was expanding rapidly and in urgent need of additional housing.

Lodge Hill Cemetery, in 1907. The cemetery serves the Selly Oak, Bournville, Weoley Hill and Weoley Castle areas, as well as adjacent suburbs. It was opened in 1895, and the original site of 17 acres has now been extended to just over 61 acres. In addition to burial grounds allocated to Anglicans, Catholics and Nonconformists, Lodge Hill has a section exclusively for Quakers, where members of the Cadbury and Lloyd families are buried. There is also a soldiers' section, where soldiers who died in local hospitals during the First World War are buried. In 1934 a chapel and crematorium were built at a cost of £9,000.

The junction of Shenley Fields Road and Castle Road, Weoley Castle, seen in 1932, showing the influence of Bournville in the spacious street layout and cottage style of the houses.

The junction of Weoley Castle Road and Princethorpe Road in 1933, shortly after completion. Such an open, sylvan setting must have come as a revelation to those previously housed in inner-city courts and terraces. This part of Weoley Castle retains much of its original character, showing why the estate was regarded as a landmark in council house building.

Weoley Castle ruins during the excavations of the early 1930s, with new housing development in the background. The present-day estate is named after a semi-fortified manor house whose ruins still survive, and whose name means 'a wood or clearing in which there is a heathen temple', though excavations have so far not revealed any evidence of other than domestic use.

A closer look at the Weoley Castle excavations, in 1932. This was the first major investigation of the site, and regular work continued until 1962. The site appears to have been occupied continuously from around 1100 until the early 1600s; it was described as a ruin around 1650, and was thereafter used as a quarry for local building stone.

A further view of the castle ruins, in 1936. The moated site was occupied by a succession of stone and timber buildings until 1380, when there was a total re-build. This resulted in a walled enclosure reached by a wooden drawbridge, with guesthouse, chapel, great hall, laundry-house, bakehouse, brewhouse, stables and kitchens.

Weoley Castle in 1932. Former lords of the manor include Paganel, Somery, Botetort, Burnell and Jerveys – all of whom are commemorated in local road names. Following the building of the Weoley Castle Estate, the ruins were opened to the public, with a small museum displaying some of the archaeologists' finds. Although the site has been closed for some years, there is currently a campaign running to re-open it.

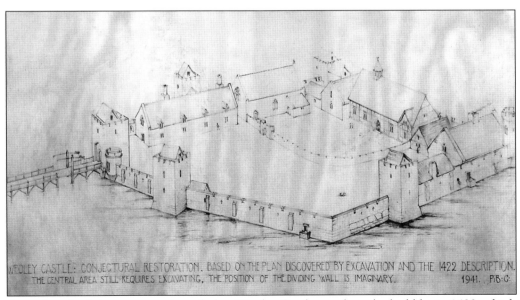

WEOLEY CASTLE: CONJECTURAL RESTORATION, BASED ON THE PLAN DISCOVERED BY EXCAVATION AND THE 1422 DESCRIPTION. THE CENTRAL AREA STILL REQUIRES EXCAVATING, THE POSITION OF THE DIVIDING WALL IS IMAGINARY.   1941. P.B.C.

An archaeologist's reconstruction of what Weoley Castle may have looked like in 1422, which was published in 1941.

Barnes Hill, showing the (now demolished) California Inn, in 1935.

Long Nuke Road, Shenley Fields, under construction in 1959.

Three
Houses and Gardens

Selly Manor, on its original site in Bournbrook Road, Selly Oak, *c*. 1890. This was prior to its removal to Bournville.

Court No. 40, Windsor Street, Birmingham, *c.* 1900. This shows the kind of confined back-to-back housing from which many of George Cadbury's adult school students came, and which he sought to replace through the example set by Bournville.

Houses in Bournville Lane, Bournville, *c.* 1910, provide a striking contrast with the preceding scene. Although such houses were beyond the reach of the poorest tenants, they were certainly attainable by skilled workers.

George Cadbury (1839-1922), son of John Cadbury, founder of the firm of Cadbury Brothers, cocoa and chocolate manufacturers, was born and bred in Edgbaston, attending a Quaker school there. He and his brother Richard took over the city firm in 1861, following their widowed father's declining health, restoring it to profitability by the mid-1860s. The firm expanded rapidly, thanks to notable innovations such as the first unadulterated cocoa, and in 1879 they moved to a healthier and more spacious site at Bournbrook, four miles to the south. The success of the new works made it likely that speculative housing developments would soon occur nearby, and to forestall these George Cadbury bought 300 acres of land adjoining the factory; he planned a model village to accommodate his own workers and others in the area seeking good-quality affordable housing. His lifelong work in adult education gave him an insight into working-class conditions at the time, and led to his stress on the great importance of education, good housing, and factory reform. He considered that good living and working conditions had a morally uplifting effect; hence the green and spacious quality of both the factory and the estate, and the excellent social welfare facilities. Educationally, his great legacies are the Bournville junior and infant schools, the College of Art, and the Selly Oak Colleges, a loose affiliation of religious studies centres, specialising in multi-faith courses, international relations, missionary work, and teacher training.

Elizabeth Cadbury (1858-1951), herself from an old Quaker family, married George Cadbury in 1888 and from the beginning assisted him in the development of Bournville. Particularly interested in the welfare of young people, she was closely associated with the YWCA, Girl Guides' Association and Union of Girls' Clubs. A major concern was the Woodlands Cripples' Hospital at Northfield, which she visited regularly. She also helped develop school medical services locally. Nationally, she worked for the Liberal Party and the National Council of Women, and – on a wider stage – for the League of Nations and the International Council of Women. She served as a councillor and a magistrate, and shared her husband's interest in adult education. Following his death in 1922, she was appointed Chairman of Bournville Village Trust, enthusiastically continuing his work till the time of her death.

Building key workers' homes in 1879. Simultaneously with the construction of the factory, twenty-four houses for key workers were erected on Bournville Lane, to the designs of George Gadd. These preceded the main village by almost twenty years, and were conventional in comparison with later Bournville designs, forming in essence the larger type of tunnel-back house, with terracotta dressings and gables.

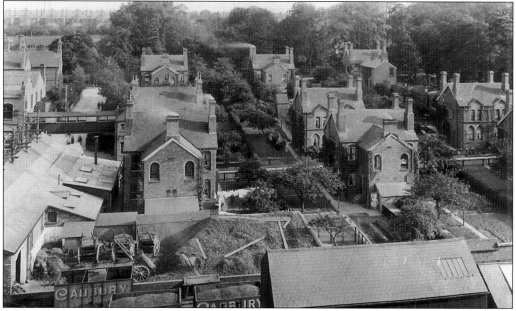

Completed key workers' houses at Bournville in 1879. An emphasis on larger than usual gardens is already apparent. For the first twenty years, most Cadbury workers lived elsewhere and walked or cycled to the factory, or travelled by train. These houses were progressively demolished as the factory expanded, the Dining Rooms block subsequently occupying the site.

Bournbrook Hall, in 1907, shortly before its demolition, formed part of the original estate purchased by George Cadbury in 1895 as the future site for his model village. Successively the property of the Izon, Stock and Martin families, it was reached by a long straight drive from Oak Tree Lane, whose line is followed by the present Linden Road. For some time it served as a hostel for Cadbury women workers who lived too far away to travel daily, and following its demolition the grounds were retained as a recreational facility for them.

The interior of Bournbrook Hall in 1906, with Cadbury women workers relaxing.

The lily pond in the Women's Recreation Grounds (or Girls' Grounds), site of the demolished Bournbrook Hall, in the 1930s. The grounds were remodelled in 1896, acquiring sporting facilities such as a gymnasium, hockey pitch, and netball and tennis courts.

Women employees relaxing in the Recreation Grounds, c. 1910. The environment is strikingly different from that enjoyed by most Edwardian factory workers.

An archway in the Women's Recreation Ground, 1949. The gardens survive in a modified form, and are now open to the public.

Bournville Almshouses, on Mary Vale Road, in 1949. They were designed by Ewan Harper for Richard Cadbury, being built 1897-98. They were intended for people over sixty, old Cadbury workers being given preference. There were thirty-three houses, each furnished and supplied with free coal, water and gas. The occupants also had medical attendance.

Each almshouse had a living room, curtained-off bedroom and kitchen, and all looked on to a central quadrangle (seen here in the 1930s), with a rest house echoing the one on the green in design. With typically Quaker 'economy of action', thirty-eight houses were built on Mary Vale Road whose rents, through an endowment, helped meet the costs of building and maintaining the almshouses.

In the gardens of Bournville Almshouses, 1912. Each tenant had an individual garden plot and there was, for a time, communal access to the orchard of the adjacent Bournbrook Hall.

William Alexander Harvey (1875-1951) was architect to the Bournville Village Trust from 1895 to 1902, and afterwards architectural consultant. He set his mark on the original village centre, designing most of the public buildings and private houses around the green. His houses, while utilising many traditional features such as half-timbering, buttressed gables, roughcast surfaces, dormer windows and leaded lights, deliberately mixed styles and periods. With a keen interest in town planning as well as architecture, he worked closely with George Cadbury to create a green and spacious setting for the houses. His harmonious 'Arts and Crafts' style was applied with equal success to large school and college buildings, and in the rebuilding of Selly Manor and Minworth Greaves he showed great talent for conservation and restoration work.

These cottages in the 'Dutch style', on Sycamore Road, Bournville, are typical of Harvey's eclectic approach to house design, forming a deliberate contrast with the comparatively plain house next door. They are seen here around 1905.

A cottage in Elm Road, showing a use of buttresses that was decorative rather than functional – a recurrent feature of Harvey's style.

A cottage on Mary Vale Road, in 1904, showing a further variation in style, this time echoing the design of the entrance lodge to a country house.

These cottages on Willow Road, again in 1904, are typical of Harvey's humbler type of house, but again show an interesting variety of window designs, no pair being exactly alike.

Another recurrent feature of Bournville is for semi-detached or terraced houses to be accommodated in a single symmetrical block that appears to be all one dwelling, as seen here on Linden Road around 1904.

Estate houses on Acacia Road,
Bournville, c. 1910.

House interior at Bournville, c.
1905.

House interior of the early 1900s.

Another house interior, *c*. 1906.

A Bournville bedroom, again *c.* 1906.

Gardening on the Woodlands Housing Association Estate in the 1930s. The Woodlands Estate consisted of 79 houses, all on 99-year leases; they were mostly sold to purchasers, all of whom were members of the society; some were let. The houses were designed by the Bournville Trust's own architects; but were built by a local builder. Gardening was highly valued by George Cadbury as a healthy recreational activity providing an alternative to the public house; it was also considered sound economically, fruit and vegetable growing being actively encouraged.

Westholme, off Oak Tree Lane, Bournville, was for many years the residence of Edward Cadbury and his wife Dorothy, followed by Henry and Lucy Cadbury. A large Victorian mansion set in extensive grounds, it was typical of several already in the area before the Cadburys built their factory. Later used as a hostel for displaced East European teenagers, it is shown here in 1965, shortly before its demolition to make way for housing developments. It is commemorated in the road name Westholme Croft.

Selly Wood, another large Victorian mansion close to Westholme, is shown here in 1967, shortly before its demolition, like Westholme, to make way for a housing estate. Its name survives in Sellywood Road, and the extensive landscaped gardens with a small lake have been largely retained as a setting for Selly Wood House, a full-time home for the elderly, and Queen Mother Court, sheltered housing for retired teachers.

Hole Farm, on Hole Lane, seen here in 1989, is one of the few surviving farmhouses in the Bournville area, although it is now a private residence with most of the farmland built on. The present building dates from the 1790s, and is probably on the site of an older house, since Hole Lane is an ancient thoroughfare, still partly a hollow way. It was for a long time the home of the Garland family (hence Garland Way), and the music hall artiste Marie Lloyd is said to have slept here as their guest. The farmland once extended to the Bristol Road; a surviving cattle pond by Garland Way has now been landscaped as part of the adjacent housing estate. The garden well was still in use as late as 1958.

Bournville Park, c. 1930. This was formerly part of the land belonging to Bournbrook Farm (later the Old Farm Hotel). Long used for the grazing of cattle, it was subsequently let to Bournville Cricket Club, who used it as their pitch until the Men's Recreation Ground at Cadbury's opened in 1896. The seven acres by the Bourn Brook were acquired by the Trust and laid out as a park in 1907, being transferred to the city in 1920. The park links the village green to the Hay Green area, and through the Valley Parkway to Weoley Hill and Weoley Castle a 'greenway' may be followed.

Selly Manor on its old site on Bournbrook Road, Selly Oak, *c.* 1890. Of fourteenth-century origin, rebuilt a century later, and subsequently extended, it was divided into three cottages in the nineteenth century, and was condemned to be demolished in the early 1900s.

In an early and far-sighted instance of conservation work, George Cadbury bought Selly Manor in 1907, had it taken down, and re-erected under the supervision of W.A. Harvey between 1912 and 1916. Every usable portion of the original fabric was included, and other contemporary building material specially collected was added as necessary. Work on the Bournville site is seen as well advanced by 1915.

Selly Manor in its restored form at Bournville, seen here in 1949. Opened as a museum in 1917, it was furnished by Laurence Cadbury, George Cadbury's son, who travelled all over England collecting suitable pieces, some dating back to around 1500. The furniture is arranged much as it might have been in the early eighteenth century, while the garden contains flowers and herbs appropriate to the period.

Bournville's second 'house that moved' is Minworth Greaves, which stands today in the grounds of Selly Manor. Originally on the Kingsbury Road between Curdworth and Minworth, to the north of Birmingham, Minworth Greaves was saved from demolition by Laurence Cadbury, who bought it in 1911. After careful survey, the timbers were numbered, removed and stored until 1929, when the house was rebuilt beside Selly Manor, again under the guidance of W.A. Harvey. Although much of the house was too decayed to be rebuilt, the present building incorporates a two-bay hall of medieval cruck construction, probably dating from the fourteenth century. Completed in 1932, the restored building is now a venue for regular and varied exhibitions. This photograph dates from 1965.

Children's playground at Laurel Grove, Bournville, c. 1910. This provided a green and spacious alternative to the streets or courts of the inner city.

Experimental houses at Hay Green Lane, Bournville, in 1920. In the early 1920s, Cadbury's and the Bournville Village Trust jointly experimented with various building materials and techniques, building several 'model' houses to illustrate these. Model homes included a Canadian type wooden bungalow, a 'rammed earth' Mediterranean type bungalow, a brick and cement bungalow, four concrete houses, a breeze block house, and a steel house. Bungalows were almost unknown in Britain at this time. These were the first Bournville homes to have purpose-built bathrooms.

Building an experimental steel house on Hay Green Lane in 1925. Not all the housing experiments were successful, the steel house having to be demolished due to condensation, and the rammed earth house later succumbing to the British climate. Nevertheless, such houses stimulated great interest, people travelling from all over the world to see them.

Self-building on Shenley Lane, *c.* 1959. By the mid-1950s, Lower Shenley farmland was beginning to be developed, 103 dwellings being planned for the first phase, to be let to families nominated by the City Council. Shenley Court Residents' Association was formed in 1952, with the village hall built by the residents themselves, the Trust providing the materials. By 1960, in co-operation with the city, 500 houses were built for corporation nominees; in addition 5 self-build housing societies were established, erecting 100 houses on the estate.

Constructing the model yachting pool in the Valley Parkway, 1932. The Valley Parkway forms a continuous linear park linking the original Bournville Village with Weoley Castle. The yachting pool was constructed by unemployed workmen who simultaneously attended educational courses provided by the Cadburys. Opened in 1933, it replaced the smaller Rowheath Pool due to the popularity of model yacht racing at the time.

The men at work on the yachting pool in 1932. The construction of the pool was characteristic of 'economy of action' on the Cadburys part, providing work for the unemployed while also enhancing the environment (reclaiming marshy ground by creating a water feature), and offering a sporting facility.

The pool in the Valley Parkway, *c.* 1950. Handed over to the City Council in 1945, the Parkway set an important precedent in that the council eventually recommended such 'greenways' as part of their own overall planning strategy.

The pool in the Valley Parkway, 1965.

Walking in the Valley Parkway, again in 1965. George Cadbury himself walked regularly through here on his way to work, handing out chocolates to children whom he met.

A drawing of houses planned for Witherford Way, Weoley Hill, published in the 1930s. Witherford Way's smaller cottage-style houses were designed by Bedford Tyler, the Trust's architect, who had drawn up plans for the whole of the Weoley Hill estate shortly before his death. Following Tyler's death, his characteristic rendered finish and slate roofs were replaced by more traditional Midland brick with clay tiles on the roofs. Witherford Way was intended for first-time buyers; hence the modest size of many of the houses.

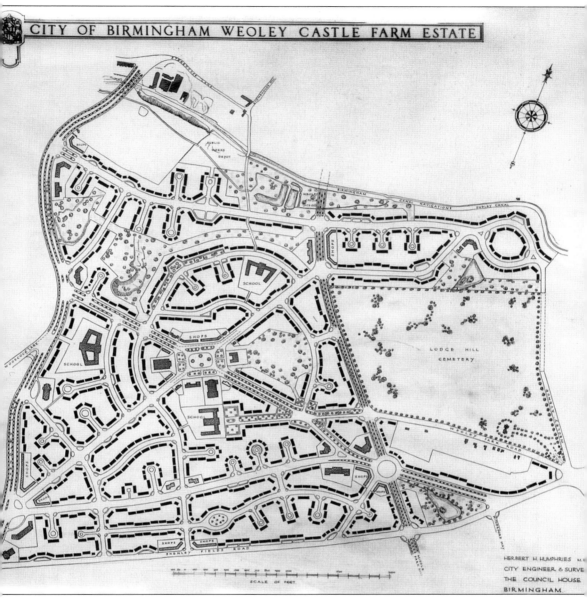

Plan for the Weoley Castle Council Estate from 1930, showing the direct influence of Bournville in the spacious layout, with wide boulevards and circles alternating with narrower winding roads, and a generous provision of public open space. As in Bournville, there are conservation features, including the preservation of a natural lake, some fields, and the medieval castle ruins. The Castle Square, a specially designated shopping centre (like Bournville Green), forms a natural focus to the estate, roads radiating from it like the spokes of a wheel.

Housing on Shenley Fields Road, 1932.

Opening of the city's 40,000th council house by Neville Chamberlain, then Chancellor of the Exchequer, on 23 October 1933, on the Weoley Castle Estate. Weoley Castle formed part of a massive council house building programme between the wars. Between 1924, when the Wheatley Housing Act was passed, and 1939, Birmingham built 50,000 council houses, more than any other local authority.

Four
Bournville Works

The first aerial view of Cadbury's Bournville Works, in 1921.

Bournville Works, shortly after opening on the new site, in 1879.

A special train bearing Cadbury's Christmas goods, Bournville, 31 October 1903. This train was used for twenty-five years.

Cadbury Works railway, *c.* 1920.

Bournville Works Dining Rooms, seen in the 1930s. They were designed by James Millar and completed in 1927. There were originally twelve separate dining rooms serving different categories of employee, changing rooms for 5,000 women workers, youth club rooms, a library, doctor's and dentist's surgeries, and a concert hall seating 1,050. More than mere dining rooms, they were the centre of social life in the factory.

Office staff arrive at the Men's Entrance in 1912. At this time, men and women were carefully segregated throughout the factory, corridors, entrances and exits being arranged so that they did not meet, and each sex was allocated separate dining rooms and recreation grounds.

Office staff arrive at the Girls' Entrance, *c.* 1908. At this time, women employees were known as 'girls' because they were mainly young unmarried women. As was customary in most firms at the time, women were obliged to resign on marrying. Women workers have, however, always played a key role at Cadbury's, particularly in wartime.

Women workers leave the Girls' Entrance, c. 1910. The prevalence of cycles in the photograph reminds us that many Cadbury employees who lived locally cycled to work at this time, there being little regular public transport, apart from the railway, in the immediate area.

Cadbury workers leave the factory, 1949.

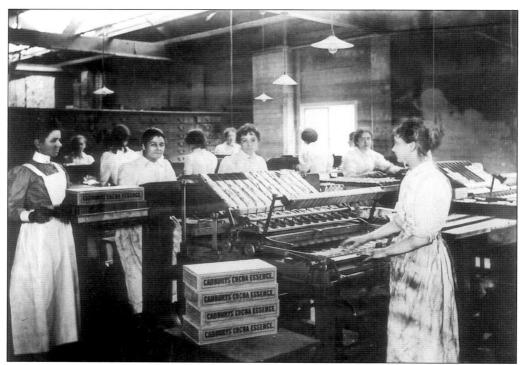

Packing cocoa essence in 1902, with Miss Griffin, the forewoman, on the left.

Wrapping chocolates in 1911.

The Despatch Department in 1907, showing direct access from the factory to the railway. Packing was in wooden boxes at this time.

The Analyst's Laboratory at Bournville Works in 1906. An analytical chemist was appointed in 1901, followed by a works doctor in 1902 and a dentist in 1905 – all evidence of the Cadburys concern for high standards in health and hygiene.

The General Office in 1912 – spacious, open-plan and top-lit, a decided contrast to Cadbury's previous Bridge Street premises.

The General Office in its new accommodation in 1921. The General Office had opened in 1879 with 8 staff; by 1920 they had around 250 staff dealing with 1,000,000 orders annually.

The Accounts Office in 1905, showing new adding machines in use. Typewriters and adding machines were the first mechanical aids adopted in the office. Cadbury's have always been responsive to new technology, as in their adoption of robots in the 1980s.

From small beginnings...The office staff in 1885, with George Cadbury and his son Edward standing to the right of the group.

The main Dining Room in 1949.

A scene in the Works Concert Hall (with the organ on the left), marking the retirement of Barrow Cadbury on 5 July 1932. Being the nephew of George Cadbury, he succeeded him as chairman of the firm in 1922, and by January 1932 he had completed 50 years of service. Over 1,000 Cadbury employees witnessed the presentation to him of a drawing of the summer-house, a gift from the staff, which had already been erected at his house, 'Southfield', Edgbaston.

The Ober-burgermeister's visit to Cadbury's, 1906.

Staff from the former works in Bridge Street, Birmingham, attend a party held at George Cadbury's home, the Manor House, Northfield, in celebration of thirty years at Bournville, September 1909. The Cadburys are seated in the centre of the front row.

Young Cadbury employees visit George Cadbury's home in 1911, with characteristic dark oak panelling and Elizabeth Cadbury's organ in the background. George Cadbury's hospitality, particularly towards young people, was legendary – not only to his own staff, but to crippled children, refugees, and many from deprived inner-city areas.

Another scene from the same visit, showing young Cadbury employees relaxing by George Cadbury's fireside in 1911.

An advertising horse van used by Cadbury's, 1910.

The last horse and cart used by the firm, Easter 1934. On the retirement of the driver, the horse and cart were sold.

Cadbury's first motor van, seen here in 1904, was one of the earliest in Birmingham. It weighed 3 tons and ran at 7 or 8mph.

A fleet of Cadbury vans in 1912. These Thorneycrofts were used throughout the First World War, one being retained after the war and winning prizes in local shows for the best-kept old vehicle.

Cadbury Company charabancs, 1920. The firm bought two charabancs for carrying visitors around the village, running a bus service for employees to and from Kings Heath, and providing transport for staff holiday tours. These were the first of their kind owned by the firm; they were later replaced by large saloon coaches.

The company charabancs, again in 1920. They provided a Kings Heath service until corporation buses were introduced.

A rail excursion to Bournville, 1929. Apart from its direct use by the firm for goods transportation, commuting, and holiday excursions, the railway saw a series of special visits arranged for Cadbury's customers, as well as day trips for interested members of the public. Public excursions ran regularly between 1929 and 1939, an estimated 50,000 coming during that period from the grocery and confectionery trades alone.

A view of the factory terrace, in 1949, showing the Dining Rooms to the right and the factory itself closing the view beyond. Although some older buildings of 1899-1902 front Bournville Lane, most of the factory as we see it today dates from the 1920s and 1930s. The Men's Recreation Ground is on the left, partly out of view.

To mark the centenary of the firm, on 28 June 1933, a fountain was presented to the management on behalf of the employees. Situated in the Men's Recreation Ground, facing the Dining Rooms, it consists of a basin and fountain of York stone, surmounted by a bronze figure of the goddess Terpsichore, the muse of choral dance and song, bearing a lyre and symbolising a hundred years of happiness and goodwill. The sculptor was William Bloye. In the background may be seen the former bridge over Bournville Lane to the Girls' Recreation Ground, and the Men's Sports Pavilion.

The Men's Recreation Ground and the factory, 1949. The phrase 'factory in a garden' was used by the firm themselves and refers to the extensive gardens and recreation grounds surrounding the factory (see also p. 91). Opened in 1896, the grounds provided facilities for football, hockey, cricket, lawn tennis and bowls.

The Sports Pavilion, in the Men's Recreation Grounds, showing the still surviving Bournbrook Hall to the right, *c.* 1905. Opened in 1902, the pavilion was a gift from Cadbury's to their male employees, in commemoration of the Coronation of Edward VII. It was built by Bedford Tyler, and is similar in general design to the contemporary factory buildings farther down the lane.

Boys' PE class, Cadbury's, *c.* 1905. The latest equipment of the day was used.

The Girls' Recreation Grounds, the former gardens of Bournbrook Hall, *c.* 1910.

The Girls' Recreation Grounds in late spring, 1925.

The Girls' Recreation Grounds, in 1949, looking past the lily pond to the walled kitchen garden. Produce from this garden supplied the works canteen, and any surplus was sold to staff.

The Girls' Swimming Baths, on Bournville Lane, c. 1910. The baths were built in 1902-04 by G.H. Lewin, and formed part of an overall fitness plan for the staff. Everyone was actively encouraged to learn to swim; there was a similar Boys' Bath. Life-saving and water ballet were also taught. The baths are currently closed, awaiting restoration.

Five

Institutions

The Beeches playing field, 1895.

St Francis' church, Bournville, in 1949. It was designed by W.A. Harvey, and completed in 1925 in a simple Romanesque style. The adjacent parish hall of 1913, also by Harvey, and linked to the church by cloisters, was used for services until the church was built. Help with funding came from members of other denominations, including Cadbury's, who in 1927 gave their former Works Dining Room organ to the church. The cloisters and vestries were completed in 1937. From the beginning, the church worked well with other denominations, enjoying especially cordial relations with the Meeting House; this is symbolised annually by the open-air carol service on the green, a joint church venture.

Weoley Hill United Reformed church, seen here shortly after completion in 1936.

The Serbian Orthodox church of St Lazar, on Cob Lane, Bournville, was the first Serbian Orthodox church to be built in this country for members of the community who had fled from Yugoslavia as political refugees at the end of the Second World War. They were later joined by members of their families, and by ex-prisoners of war. The Serbians have been associated with Bournville since the First World War, when Dame Elizabeth Cadbury was involved in the care and education of thirty Serbian refugee children. Many of the exiled Serbs secured jobs at Cadbury's. Designed in the Serbian Byzantine style, the church is the exact replica of one in Yugoslavia, and was built with stone from the same quarries, largely by the congregation themselves. The church is seen here shortly after completion in 1968.

The interior of St Lazar's church, 1969. Reached by an entrance door of hand-beaten copper panels, it contains a fourteenth-century wooden screen, a giant metal chandelier symbolising the Divine Crown, and a huge painted figure of Christ covering the main dome and surrounded by frescoes of twelve Old Testament prophets.

The Friends' Meeting House, Bournville, in 1949. It was built in 1905 to the design of W.A. Harvey for the accommodation of 400 people, and is highly unusual for a Quaker place of worship in having an organ. There were several reasons for this. George Cadbury, himself a keen musician, wanted more structured Quaker meetings, incorporating hymns and prayers, particularly in the early days of Bournville, when the Meeting House was the only local place of worship and non-Quakers also attended. He also wanted the Meeting House to be a true community centre, accessible to local people during the week, and wanted the organ to be used for concerts – a role it still fulfils.

The Friends' Meeting House in the 1970s. George Cadbury's ashes are buried here, along with those of other Quakers, and his bust looks out from an alcove over the village green he created. An evergreen, planted in the grounds in 1948 by Elizabeth Cadbury, was for many Christmases decorated with coloured lights, its prominent hilltop position making it an impressive roadside attraction.

The interior of the Friends' Meeting House in the 1930s.

Bournville Infants' School, on the green, completed in 1910, was designed by W.A. Harvey, and was – like its junior school neighbour – the gift of George and Elizabeth Cadbury. It has architectural features suggesting a small-scale Tudor manor, no doubt reflecting Harvey's simultaneous preoccupation with the rebuilding of Selly Manor, soon to face it across the green. In a characteristic touch, the foundation stone was laid by George Cadbury's young daughter Ursula, herself of infant school age. The school was extended in 1938. It is seen here in 1965.

A pupil on the balcony of the infants' school assembly hall, 1911.

Bournville Junior School, c. 1960. It was built in 1906 for 540 children, six classrooms for 50 children each, and six for 40. The central hall contains sixteen frescoes depicting scenes from the New Testament on specially prepared cement panels. The carillon topping the school tower dates, in its present form, from 1934. In the early days of the schools, the carillon played hymn tunes appropriate to the arrival and departure of the children: 'New every morning is the love' and 'Now the day is over'.

Gardening at Bournville Junior School in 1986 – a new generation helping to maintain Bournville's renowned 'green' tradition.

PE in the assembly hall at Bournville Junior School in 1921. The New Testament frescoes, by Mrs Creighton McDowell and Mary Sargant Florence, can be clearly seen on the upper walls.

Ruskin Hall, Bournville Green, in 1949. The hall adjoins the junior school, forming part of W.A. Harvey's Neo-Tudor educational complex. Completed in 1903, largely at the expense of George and Elizabeth Cadbury, it began as a social centre, later housing the temporary infants' school. It became a school of arts and crafts following the absorption of Bournville by Birmingham in 1911. The building was extended in 1927/28, 1946 and 1958.

The Day Continuation School, Bournville Green, in 1949. It was built in 1925 in response to Fisher's Education Act of 1918, which was intended to provide a national system of part-time education for those leaving school at fourteen. Very few such schools were built; but Cadbury's long-standing interest in the education of their employees – they maintained an excellent works library – made Bournville a natural choice for implementing this pioneering day-release scheme.

Students leaving classes at the Day Continuation School in the 1930s. At the time of opening, there were 1,850 students, and by 1935 five firms and two council departments were making use of the facilities offered. In 1949, the school became a college, and by 1953 there were sixty employers using its facilities, sending staff mostly for one whole day a week. In 1973, due to pressure on space, the college was annexed to the School of Arts and Crafts, and new premises (the present Bournville College) were built on Bristol Road.

A class at the Day Continuation School, not long after opening, in 1925. Taking the class is Mr C.J.V. Bews, head of the college from its inception until his retirement in 1946. For Cadbury employees, classes were compulsory for the under eighteens until 1971. The aim of the school was not to give a specific technical or professional training, but to continue the general education of the young workers. The curriculum included physical training and English, and students had a choice of subjects in the arts, crafts and sciences. It was hoped they would acquire the rudiments of good citizenship and discover some worthwhile hobby or an interest of lasting value.

Bournville Boys' Technical School (1955) and Bournville Girls' (1954) opened on Griffins Brook Lane to cater for the senior age group. By 1970, each was referred to as a grammar/technical school. In 1973, the two schools merged, and are now known as Bournville School. The boys' school is seen here in 1957.

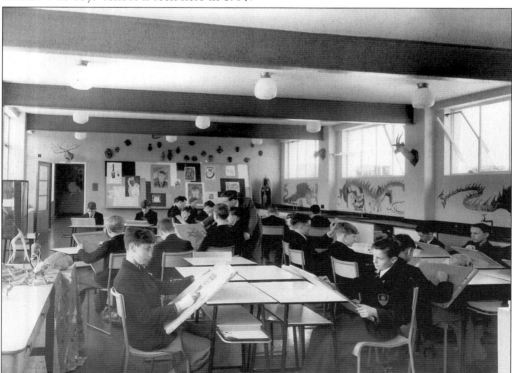

The Art Room at Bournville Boys' Technical School in 1957.

Green Meadow Junior School, Shenley Fields, seen soon after its opening in 1958.

Inside Green Meadow Junior School, *c.* 1958.

Dame Elizabeth Cadbury School, Woodbrooke Road, Bournville, in 1965. This began as a secondary modern in 1951, and now serves as a comprehensive secondary school and sixth form centre.

Woodbrooke College, *c.* 1960. Lying just off Bristol Road, between Bournville and Weoley Hill, it is of eighteenth-century origin, but was remodelled in 1830 by the pen manufacturer Josiah Mason, who later founded Birmingham University. The property passed to the Elkington family in 1839, and was the home of George Cadbury between 1881 and 1894. In accordance with his wishes, it was opened in 1903 as a Quaker study centre, concerned with biblical and theological studies, and peace, reconciliation and social issues. Residential and short courses, and conferences with a Quaker emphasis, are offered, as well as the opportunity for spiritual retreats. The earliest of the Selly Oak Colleges, it is noted for its library and extensive conservation garden.

The Missionary Guest House, Selly Oak, designed by Beresford Pite, in a drawing of 1926. It is now the Methodist Overseas Guest House. The Selly Oak Foundation claim to instil in their students 'a wholeness of view on what human life is about and knowing the entire world-wide human community as the horizon for any particular sphere of service': hence the emphasis on international concerns in all the colleges.

Kingsmead College, designed by W.A. Harvey and seen here in the 1920s, was founded in 1905 as a missionary college by the Methodist Church Overseas Division.

The old buildings of Fircroft College, on Oak Tree Lane, Bournville, are seen here in 1957, shortly before transfer to the new premises on Bristol Road, Selly Oak. First mentioned in 1841, this was originally a private house known as Dell Cottage, and was bought by George Cadbury in 1909. He turned it into a working men's college, closely associated with the W.E.A., the trade unions, and the Co-operative Movement.

The new buildings at Fircroft College, shortly after opening in 1957. Formerly known as Primrose Hill, this house was for some years the home of George Cadbury Jnr, son of George Cadbury, and following his death, suitably altered and extended, was opened as the new college premises.

A class at Fircroft College, also in 1957. Year-long courses have included economics, literature, peace studies, philosophy, politics, maths and sociology.

Studying at Fircroft College, again in 1957, the Bournville influence is apparent in the wide windows commanding extensive views of the attractive wooded grounds, a feature of all the Selly Oak Colleges.

The former Fircroft College, on Oak Tree Lane, is now the estate office of the Bournville Village Trust. It is seen here in 1958.

Founded and sponsored by the major Free Churches in 1907, Westhill College (seen here around 1930) was designed by W.A. Harvey, and is now (like the other Selly Oak Colleges) affiliated to the University of Birmingham. It specialises in religious teacher training, youth and community work, church education and management, and pastoral studies. There were major extensions to the building in the 1960s.

The College of the Ascension, *c.* 1930. It was founded in 1923 by the United Society for the Propagation of the Gospel. Other Selly Oak study centres include the Centre for New Religious Movements, the Multi-Faith Centre, and the Centre for Black and White Christian Partnership.

Carey Hall, designed by W.A. Harvey, was founded in 1912 for the training of women missionaries. It is seen here around 1930. More recent foundations include Prospect Hall (1978), sponsored by the City of Birmingham Social Services, and intended to foster greater independence in the physically handicapped, and Springdale (1981), a theological college for laity and ministers-in-training.

The George Cadbury Memorial Hall, soon after its opening in 1927. It was designed in a Neo-Georgian style by Hubert Lidbetter. The gift of Dame Elizabeth Cadbury, it serves the Selly Oak Colleges' community as an assembly hall.

Building the community hall at Shenley Manor in 1958. The hall was built by members of the local community.

The Beeches, Selly Oak Road, Bournville, in the 1920s. It was built for George and Elizabeth Cadbury in 1908, and was originally intended to provide holiday accommodation for children from inner-city areas; it was used in the winter months by women from the Salvation Army – a movement whose social concerns were much admired by George Cadbury.

The Beeches in 1906. It has served several functions, being used as a war hospital 1914-18, and then housing Cadbury girls' Day Continuation classes. Between the wars, it served as a residential training centre for unemployed women. During the Second World War, it housed staff and students of Hillcroft Working Women's College, and then became a hostel for Birmingham University students. Later used by Cadbury's as a college for grocers, it is now a management training centre.

Dame Elizabeth Hall, Oak Tree Lane, Bournville, was built in 1958/59 in memory of Dame Elizabeth Cadbury. It is used for committee meetings, as well as larger meetings, parties, receptions and entertainments. It is seen here in 1985.

Six
Events

The Maypole Dance at Cadbury's Children's Festival, *c.* 1905.

To commemorate the Silver Wedding Anniversary of George and Elizabeth Cadbury (on 19 June 1913), the Cadbury workforce worldwide presented the couple with the Rest House on Bournville Green. In this photograph, we see E.S. Thackray handing over the Rest House on behalf of the employees. George and Elizabeth Cadbury are standing behind the table, on either side of H.E. Johnson (seated). To the left in the photograph, facing the camera, is Clara Davis, George Cadbury's secretary, while members of the Cadbury family are standing at the rear.

George and Elizabeth Cadbury leave the Rest House after the presentation ceremony. With them is their daughter Ursula, who proved to be their longest surviving child, dying recently at the age of ninety-five.

114

Bournville's most notable royal visit was on 21 May 1919, when George V and Queen Mary toured the village in the afternoon, following their opening of the new Birmingham Children's Hospital in the morning. The King presented military decorations to a number of local ex-servicemen, and was then regaled in the Girls' Grounds by a massed choir of 4,000 white-clad women workers.

The King and Queen then proceeded to Bournville Almshouses on Mary Vale Road, where they were introduced to the oldest resident, Mrs Tutin, aged ninety-six, whose father had driven the Royal Mail Coach for George IV. After receiving presentation boxes of Cadbury's chocolates, the King and Queen toured the village, making a personal call at No. 88 Linden Road, the home of Mr A.R. Mansfield.

George Cadbury died, aged eighty-three, at the Manor House, Northfield, on 24 October 1922. Following cremation at Perry Barr on 28 October, a memorial service was held on the village green, Bournville, attended by a crowd of over 16,000 people.

Barrow Cadbury opening Rowheath Pavilion on 11 June 1924. In 1915, some 70 acres of land had been purchased to provide additional playing fields for Cadbury employees; but the war delayed development till the early 1920s. Nine acres were allotted to a gardening club, and there was a large lawn for dancing and open-air concerts, and a model yachting lake. Football and rugby, hockey, cricket, tennis, bowls, clock-golf and croquet were all catered for. A new road across the recreation ground (Heath Road) connected the old and new parts of the village.

To mark his retirement from the chairmanship of the firm on 5 July 1932, Barrow Cadbury was presented with a summer-house by the employees.

The presentation of a fountain by the employees to the Cadbury management on 28 June 1933 marked the centenary of the foundation of the firm.

Elizabeth Cadbury plants a tree on 12 May 1937, to commemorate the Coronation of George VI.

Celebrations for the Coronation of George VI, held at Bournville in 1937, show a procession passing Selly Manor.

The visit of George VI and Queen Elizabeth to Bournville in 1939. The King had previously visited in 1929, when he was the Duke of York.

Children's party at Bournville, held on VJ Day, 15 August 1945.

The visit of Queen Elizabeth and the Duke of Edinburgh to Cadbury's in 1955. The royal car stopped only briefly at the Concert Hall; but the couple were greeted with a great many flags and flowers and much cheering, and were presented with a special casket.

The consecration, by Bishop Firmilijan, of the foundation stone of St Lazar's Serbian Orthodox church, Bournville, 12 September 1965. It was designed by the Serbian architect Dragomir Tadic in the traditional style of the Morava school of the fourteenth century.

Seven
Leisure and Sport

Dancing in the Girls' Grounds at Cadbury's in 1921 – a tradition continued throughout the inter-war years.

Festival dance at Weoley Hill, 1951.

Tug o'war at the Children's Festival, Bournville, in the 1950s.

Bournville Cricket Team, 1887, with, Arthur Lilley (who later played for Warwickshire) to the left of the group, and William A. Cadbury on the far right. The original cricket pitch at Cadbury's was regarded as one of the best in the Midlands, producing a number of well-known players. Several members of the Cadbury family were themselves enthusiastic sportsmen.

Cadbury's office walk, 1939. The walk started from the sports pavilion.

Rowheath Pavilion, 1949. In recent years, 65 acres of the original sports grounds at Rowheath have been built on, resulting in the provision of both privately owned dwellings and several housing schemes for the elderly and needy. The remaining playing fields, however, continue to be well used, and there is increasing general public use of the pavilion for fashion shows, art exhibitions, circus, jazz and folk evenings, craft fairs, and band concerts.

The model yachting pool behind Rowheath Pavilion, in the 1920s. Bournville Model Yacht Club was initially based at Rowheath; but moved to the Valley Parkway in 1933 on the completion of a specially constructed lake and boathouse there. It enjoys a high standing nationally.

The Valley Parkway and pool, seen in 1970, with still undeveloped meadows beyond.

Model yachtsmen at the Valley
Parkway Pool, 1976.

Motorcycle rally at Cadbury's, 1922.

The Old Farm Inn, Bournville, *c.* 1910. Originally known as Bournbrook Farm and of eighteenth-century origin, its best-known resident was Sarah Froggatt, who lived there from 1864 to 1899 and became well-known as a herbalist, treating Cadbury workers for ailments and injuries before they had their own works doctor. Following Mrs Froggatt's death, the architect W.A. Harvey remodelled it as a traditional village inn, but at the Trust's request it remained a temperance tavern. In recent years, the Old Farm has acquired a drinks licence for meals, and the Cadbury staff clubs now serve alcohol; otherwise, Bournville remains 'dry'.

Gardening on the Woodlands Estate, Bournville, in the 1930s – an archetypal Bournville image, with a man gardening beneath his apple trees while his daughters lie reading on the grass, all three productively engaged. The Bournville Village Trust planted fruit trees at the bottom of gardens when they were first laid out; such careful siting helped to make the gardens private. As an estate manager, the Trust was unusual in not only partly planting gardens, but also in hiring out tools and offering practical instruction in gardening.

Playing bowls in the Men's Recreation Ground at Cadbury's, 1949.

Maypole dancing at Bournville Children's Festival, held on the Men's Recreation Ground at Cadbury's in 1910. George Cadbury founded the Bournville Festival in 1902, considering it an appropriate event for a traditional village community. The maypole dance has always been a key feature of the festival, which survives to the present day, still concluding with a firework display.

The Maypole Dance in 1974.